Painting Manchester's Pubs

by Michael John Ashcroft

With thanks to all those friends who have given their time, thoughts and feelings towards their favourite pubs, and my friend Heather (PH Gallery) for all her valuable help.

ISBN: 978-1-911138-20-4

Published by Nu-Age Print & Copy
289 Padiham Road, Burnley, Lancs. BB12 0HA

Painting Manchester's Pubs

I have always been fascinated by pubs. The smell, the look, the atmosphere and of course the beer.

It seemed obvious that I would always end up painting one or two, or as it turned out lots!!

I have painted all around the country, but nothing gives me more satisfaction than a top Manchester Ale House, it's probably because of the friendly warm feeling they give off and not forgetting the fine ales they produce up north.

I have decided to put a collection of paintings together of my favourite Manchester pubs, along with quotes given to me by friends in this little book which will hopefully bring lots of pleasure and nostalgic memories to whom ever reads it, over a pint of course.....

Cheers!!!!   Michael

End of The Line 12 x 28

Biography

Michael John Ashcroft M.A.F.A

Born in 1969, Michael John Ashcroft grew up in a small village called Croston in the heart of Lancashire. After leaving school in 1985, Michael began his career as an engineer, painting and sketching only in his spare time. In 1998 Michael had a major operation to remove a brain tumour, then he decided to paint more seriously. He returned back to college and completed numerous classes including A Level Fine Art.

Michael's paintings have evolved over the years from early abstract acrylics, to using oils and more representational works painted on location. The foundations that underpin his paintings hasn't changed, that is his fascination with light and dark, together with his love for the city and the landscape.

"There are no secrets in what he does. Being open and honest he tells you directly through his pictures where his interests lie. We don't have to be told by experts the meaning of his work because they are self-evident – we can see them for ourselves. In his landscapes as well as his views of the city, he willingly lays bare his pleasures and beliefs. You can't ask more of any artist than this. He is a worthy heir of those in the great tradition of Lancashire painters".

David Lee (Art Critic)

Castle Hotel

66 Oldham Street

10 x 8

"The Castle Hotel has claimed many an afternoon, lying precariously on the route between my old Shudehill studio and Piccadilly Station. An old dark wood bar and barstools that wouldn't look out of place in New York's East Village, the best jukebox in town AND live music after dark make it one of my favourite pubs in Manchester."

Ian Mood (Artist)

Abel Heywood

Northern Quarter

8 x 10

"A must do on a trip to Manchester, the Abel Heywood is a characterful pub and hotel in the heart of the Northern Quarter. Good food, local and wider craft beers and of course a fine selection of gins - what more could you want except your good friends there with you too."

Andrea Ashton (NHS Pharmacy Manager)

Afternoon Break

The Wonder Inn

12 x 10

"Alas gone, but not forgotten…..

The Wonder Inn, a quirky bar which I managed to capture just before it disappeared forever."

Michael J Ashcroft (Artist)

Ape and Apple

25 x 35

"This is an early painting of mine and it was one of the largest I had done up to that date. I completed a few sketches and took photographs with the street and pub lights on, so I could work back in the studio. This painting was definitely influenced by Edward Hopper, whose work has inspired me over the years."

Michael J Ashcroft (Artist)

Atlas Bar

10 x 10

"The inspiration for this painting was of course the Blue neon lights, not forgetting the amazing choice of gins too! I added the dark car to give the painting perspective and also more contrast."

Michael J Ashcroft (Artist)

Cask

8 x 10

"Cask is a small gem of a bar which was opened in 2009, to be found across the road from the Science & Industry Museum. Loads of choice of European beers, a great place to stop off for a thirsty pint when finished in the Museum."

Michael J Ashcroft (Artist)

Churchill's

8 x 10

"Churchill's at the end of Canal Street, that's if you make it that far what with all the bars along the way….."

Michael J Ashcroft (Artist)

Circus Tavern 1790

11 x 9

"Circus Tavern is a wonderful little gem of a pub. Had a wonderful night in there with Michael Palin many years ago."

Tony Husband (Cartoonist)

Corner of Mother Macs

11 x 8

"I couldn't let this old traditional Manchester Ale House pass me by, It had to be on my list of pubs to paint. It wasn't an easy task though it has to be said. I couldn't get an angle on it as it's quite closed in, but I found the right spot in the end, hence the title. Renamed Mother Macs in 1969 after a former Landlady, and reputed to be one of the most haunted Pubs in Manchester."

Michael J Ashcroft (Artist)

Deansgate Viaduct

9 x 12

"It's a pub that feels like home to me, warm, happy and always welcoming. A great place to have a drink with friends and family."

Marcus Whittle (Art Collector)

Dogs Allowed, Briton's Protection

20 x 20

"Britons Protection, the pub which has played host to some of Manchester's most famous and respected musicians, the keeper of secrets, where battles have been lost and won over a pint."

Rob Hefferan (Artist)

Picture In My Mind, Briton's Protection

20 x 20

Dressed In Black

10 x 10

"One of my all-time drinking establishments, there cannot be a more welcoming place on Earth on a cold winter's night than Sam's Chop House. A pub I have had the pleasure of frequenting since first arriving in Manchester as a student from the right side of the Pennines back in 1992, at which point it had already been serving the people of Manchester the finest beers, wines and food for 120 years! What a better place for an art lover to sit and enjoy a pint than at LS Lowry's favourite pub - with the stunning bronze statue of the great man himself! His drink was always a half pint of Wilson's bitter, the cask ale served in Sam's until 1990...mine's always a pint of Guinness."

Howard C. Ratcliffe (Property Businessman & Philanthropist)

Drive By On Tib Lane

10 x 10

"I was admiring the orange glow and looking for an excuse to paint the Town Hall Tavern again when a car screeched around the corner, the headlights glared in my eyes and reflected off the damp road in front, there it was, a seed planted and another painting set in motion, that's all it takes sometimes."

Michael J Ashcroft (Artist)

Brown's Pickup

16 x 16

"Formerly a bank designed by Charles Heathcote in 1902 the stunning architecture and exquisite interior makes this one of Manchester's most iconic buildings. As I was contemplating how I was going to construct the painting, a taxi pulled up at the front entrance and straight away the title came to me. Brown's Pickup, sometimes a title comes first when I'm working on a new painting and this can lead me in a direction or composition I might not have seen before."

Michael J Ashcroft (Artist)

Pint? Gas Lamp

10 x 8

"A great pub for an afternoon pint is the Gas Lamp on Bridge Street, a subterranean haven for beer lovers, the perfect place to catch up with friends during the dark winter months."

Ben Kelly (Artist)

Lower Turks Head

8 x 10

"What a nostalgic and historic pub. Walking in, you are greeted with a long bar and friendly staff, take a pew, whilst watching footie on the telly. A pub to relax and chill in. The secret I don't tell anyone about is the 'Rooftop Terrace', a small but cosy space, which if you are lucky to find a seat is a great place to spend an hour sketching."

Michael J Ashcroft (Artist)

Mackie Mayors

8 x 10

"Many covetous eyes were cast in Altrincham's direction when Nick and Jenny Johnson opened their curated market in the town centre. They followed that with the Mackie Mayor in Manchester City centre and we covet no more. They have each given life to either moribund or desolate districts by using buildings for their original purposes, purveying food."

Howard Sharrock (Nordoff Robbins)

Marble Arch By Night

9 x 12

"The Marble is everyman's ideal of a classic Manc pub. From the moment you glimpse the original tiles or take a first sip of winter ale on the way to watch a City match you know you are standing in a church of the authentic. If you are seeking refuge from the rain in a quiet corner or a quick pint with an arm round an old friend or the best pub grub in town…. it's The Marble."

Neal Keeling (M.E.N Chief Reporter)

Marble Arch

10 x 10

"The Marble Arch is a place I always return to whenever I am in Manchester. This pub introduced me to the delights of Earl Grey IPA for which I will be forever grateful. A proper pub with a great interior and even better beers! This is a must visit drinking establishment, and the food is pretty good too!"

Brian Woan (Beer Expert)

Night and Day

16 x 12

"I've always felt a real affinity with the Night and Day. I played there with the Clint Boon Experience in the late 90's (with Alfie Boe as 'Opera Dude' on backing vocals). I've DJ'd there many times and interviewed bands in the basement for various radio shows I've presented over the years. To me, the Night and Day is and always has been at the heart of Manchester's music scene in every way. "

Clint Boon (DJ and Musician)

No Room at the Inn,

Mr Thomas's Chop House

8 x 10

"Manchester's First Chop House. Opened by chef Thomas Studd in 1887, when this location faced the city's original Town Hall. If only these walls could speak."

Roger Ward (Chop House owner)

Oyster Bar

8 x 10

"On a summer weekend you won't find a busier bar, this quaint old building is a magnet for shoppers and visitors alike looking for liquid refreshment, good food, and to soak up the ambience and relax in the middle of town."

Michael J Ashcroft (Artist)

Passing The Anchor

8 x 10

"The Crown and Anchor situated in the Northern Quarter was definitely at the top of the list to be painted. I had to wait for the right light, but it was well worth it. The warm hues and painterly approach made it a joy to work on; needless to say a pint afterwards finished the job!"

Michael J Ashcroft (Artist)

Peveril of the Peak

12 x 16

"When I first came to Manchester I saw that pub and it looked so traditional and yet picturesque and inviting. It is quintessentially Manchester to me and it has never changed . As such when I see it I know I am home and life is good."

Tony Heagerty (Professor Manchester Royal Infirmary)

The Right Side of the Pev

8 x 11

"If I had to choose one pub, it would have to be the Peveril. For the way it looks, (all gorgeous green tiles), the fact that its still family run, and for all the memories of happy evenings spent in its cosy rooms, playing table football, drinking good ale when it was hard to find and putting the world to rights."

Liam Spencer (Artist)

Summer Downpour

10 x 8

Sam's Bar

10 x 10

"Sam's is one of Manchester's most iconic pubs, and is almost 150 years old, but it has its own place in the history of art in the city. LS Lowry was a regular here in the 1960s and is immortalised in the bar by a fine life-sized bronze by Peter Hodgkinson, RA."

Roger Ward (Chop House Owner)

Saturday Afternoon At The Kettle

8 x 10

"This pub has definitely seen some history, that's for sure! What with fires, and scuffles between united and city fans, its certainly had its fair share but it has to be said its certainly come out the other side. Stands proud on the junction of Great Ancoats Street and Oldham Road it's a must for any real ale lover."

Michael J Ashcroft (Artist)

Patiently Waiting

24 x 18

"I love all of Michael's work and this one is hung in my dining room so I can view it regularly. I love the light reflected on the pub sign and the reflection of the opposite building on the upstairs windows. That is his dog Murphy "Patiently Waiting" at the door, what a delight!"

Kevin Nicholson (Art Collector)

Sunbathing, Lass O' Gowrie

10 x 8

"This has to be one of my favourites. I remember sitting in here with all my mates before venturing out to Manchester Academy to see the next up and coming band. Fond memories indeed!"

Michael J Ashcroft (Artist)

The Lion

10 x 8

"Located just off Deansgate, a great place to watch the match on a Saturday afternoon... This is a recent painting and one I was really pleased with, some paintings just work, whatever you throw at them and this was one of those! The light was just right and the composition was perfect even down to the lamp post on the left, which stops your eye wandering off the edge. I added the lady with the red scarf just to give some perspective and a focal point."

Michael J Ashcroft (Artist)

Town Hall Tavern By Night

8 x 10

"Tucked away on Tib Lane is a little gem of a pub. I have painted this view a few times, even getting the Town Hall clock in appearing above the rooftops and it never disappoints. I always seem to do a nocturne painting though, I think it's because it looks so appealing every time I see it with the lights on. The orange glow against the dark imposing buildings that surrounds it, a painter's dream for me who's always looking for strong lights and darks."

Michael J Ashcroft (Artist)

The Rising Sun

10 x 8

"Michael's painting of The Rising Sun – one of Manchester's oldest pubs – is full of character and charm. Through Michael's understanding of light, he perfectly captures the reflection of the early morning sun in the pub's windows, and the reflections of the pub façade on the wet pavement."

Alex Reuben (Contemporary Six)

The Salutation

8 x 10

"A favourite Manchester pub of mine is the Salutation in Hulme, my dad grew up living across the road from it. It's a Manchester institution, the surroundings have changed over time, but the pub remains as solid as ever, serving locals and thirsty scholars."

Ben Kelly (Artist)

The Sawyers Arms

8 x 10

"Michael Ashcroft's 'Sawyer's Arms' displays all the hallmarks of his particularly English vision. The quality of Englishness lies most obviously in the choice of subject and the convincing effect of sunlight after rain. To my mind, it also resides in the restraint the artist has exercised in handling subtle blocks of colour and in the delicately descriptive marks punctuating the whole scene."

Norman Long MAFA (Artist)

The Smithfield Tavern

8 x 10

"Located in an area which seems to be forever in a state of flux, this pub succeeds in being true to its origins whilst simultaneously being at the vanguard of Manchester's burgeoning craft brewery scene. In a testament to the essence of the pub, it melds the traditional with the modern and yet achieves this without any recourse to faux nostalgia or corporate branding. As a result, the pub exudes a warmth and authenticity which engenders a spirit of genuine conviviality."

John Hadfield (Art Collector)

The Unicorn

8 x 10

"My favourite pub is The Unicorn in the Northern Quarter. This is a proper old-fashioned multi-roomed pub that's been going strong for two hundred years, although rebuilt in the 1920s. It's got an island bar so big you could live in it and has panelling that's a treat to the eye. With hidden nooks and crannies and 'colourful' locals, plus live music this is a stalwart institution ruled by the glorious landlady, Kirsten. "

Mr Jonathan G Schofield (Editor, Writer & Tour Guide)

Union Of The Bee,

New Union

8 x 10

"This pub highlighted the Manchester bee just recently which has been a symbol of solidarity in the city for more than 150 years and even more so with the recent attack on Manchester Arena. We all know someone who has "The Bee" tattoo (including my daughter Jess). I have painted this pub before but never with bees!"

Michael J Ashcroft (Artist)

The White Lion

10 x 8

"Strong cool shadows and warm greens was my inspiration for this painting. I also liked the reflection in the window from the sky, which breaks up the darks on the left side. I was also looking for a focal point down the street, when a chap kindly walked up; needless to say I put him in."

Michael J Ashcroft (Artist)

<u>Society Member</u>
Manchester Academy of Fine Art
<u>Awards</u>
Royal Institute of Oil Painters, Winner of the Frank Herring Easel Award 2017
BoldBrush Award 2017 Winner, Buxton Spa Prize 3rd Prize 2015
BoldBrush Award, Finalist 2014, Artist of the Year 2013 Highly Commended
Artist of the Year 2013 Finalist, International Artist Finalist
Brownedge Art Festival Winner, West Lancashire Open Commendation
South Ribble Winner and Peoples Prize, Harris Museum Winner 2009
Show Me The Monet Finalist
<u>Exhibitions</u>
Contemporary Six Solo Exhibition 2018
McGill Duncan Art Gallery 2016, 2017, 2018,
New Light Exhibition Tullie House Museum and Art Gallery 2018
New Light Exhibition Bankside Gallery, London 2018,
New Light Exhibition Huddersfield Art Gallery 2018
Contemporary Six Gallery 2017, Colourfield Gallery 2017
New Light Exhibition Bowes Museum 2017, Royal Institute of Oil Painters, London 2017
Buxton Spa Prize 2015, 2016, Royal Institute of Oil Painters, London 2011, 2012, 2014
Royal Society of British Artists 2014
Thompson's Art Gallery, Marylebone, Exhibition 2014
Artist Of The Year Exhibition 2014 Mall Galleries, London
MAFA Spring Exhibition 2013, Harris open Exhibition 2013
John Noott Joint Exhibition 2013
Thompson's Art Gallery, Marylebone Autumn Exhibition 2013
Biscuit Factory Art Gallery, Newcastle Autumn Exhibition 2013
Hepplestones Fine Art Gallery 2013, Howard De Walden Exhibition, London 2012, 2013,
Hepplestones Fine Art Gallery Solo Exhibition 2012
Colourfield Gallery Visions of Manchester Joint Exhibition 2012